A Voice of Her Own

A Voice of Her Own

The Story of Phillis Wheatley, Slave Poet

KATHRYN LASKY

ILLUSTRATED BY PAUL LEE

CANDLEWICK PRESS
2067 MASSACHUSETTS AVENUE
CAMBRIDGE MA 02140

"Snatched from Afric's Fancy'd Happy Seat"

At first there was just blackness. Complete blackness. Then the blackness dissolved into darkness, and the world in the creaking hold of the slave ship slid with shadows. The air reeked. The little girl could pick out shapes—shapes of men, women, and children; most from Senegambia, on the west coast of Africa.

She also saw the scurrying shapes of rats and the dark gleam of chains. All the men were chained. The slave ship had slipped from that African shore in the dead of night. If the slaves had seen their homeland disappearing over the horizon, if they had understood what was happening, they might have jumped into the sea despite their chains.

She heard chains now, overhead. Some of the men had been taken onto the deck to dance. They were all made to dance every day to the thin whine of a pipe. Without the dancing their limbs grew stiff, their muscles weak. This would be bad. The cargo would be less valuable. The girl shut her eyes. In her mind another picture grew.

The darkness was replaced with the amber light of dawn. In the place of shadows walked a solitary figure, her cloth wrap fluttering in the breeze. She carried a bowl made from a calabash gourd. She kneeled; then raising her arms to the sun, she let water spill from the gourd to the ground. The woman was her mother. She made the daily offering to welcome the sun. The girl would never see her mother again, but she would keep the picture of her mother, the sun, and the spilling water forever in her mind. She would treasure it as if it were the most precious jewel. She would also try to remember the palms, the gleaming calabashes, and the endless fields of elephant grass.

"We'll Call Her Phillis"

After nearly ten weeks at sea, the schooner had arrived in Boston Harbor and tied up at the Beach Street Wharf. It was a summer day in 1761. The slaves had been cleaned and greased to make their black skin glisten. However, the ship's owner, Mr. Fitch, glowered at what he saw. "A mean cargo," he muttered under his breath. He meant that there were too many women and children, and not enough strong young males who would sell at a high price. John Avery, the agent who had arranged the sale, was nervous, too. He immediately put a very low price on the small naked girl who stood shivering, clutching a scrap of carpet to her body. He reckoned her to be about seven years old, as she was missing two front teeth. She looked weak. He doubted that she would last through the harsh New England winter.

A handsomely dressed man and woman stood in front of her, discussing her with the agent, but the English words were a blur to her ears.

Susannah Wheatley had been looking for a somewhat older girl to be her servant, but this frail creature would have to do. Besides, there was something that touched her about the modest way the girl stood with her scrap of carpet. Her face was interesting.

The girl was bought for a few dollars, and the woman led her down the wharf to the waiting carriage.

"What will you call her?" John Wheatley asked his wife.

Susannah hesitated, but as the carriage pulled away, she looked back at the ship on which the girl had come. The name *Phillis* was written on the stern.

"Phillis . . . we'll call her Phillis."

Everything looked and smelled strange. The scents of tar and turpentine wafted from the ships and the docks. And from one building, its doors open, came the strong smell of rum. Then, as the carriage pulled by a market, the smell of tea rolled out like a huge cloud. Soon, however, the tea cloud vanished, replaced by the odor of fish. Phillis had never smelled so much fish.

Most of the faces of the people around her were white, but there were some tan and some yellow-brown and some black. The man who drove the carriage was black. Everyone moved fast, even the ladies in their long full skirts. Boston was the strangest sight Phillis had ever seen.

The carriage stopped in front of a large red-brick mansion on the corner of King and Mackerel Streets.

New England slaves were treated differently from Southern slaves. Life was somewhat easier, physically. But never had a New England slave been treated like Phillis. Susannah Wheatley had originally wanted a personal servant but quickly saw that she had someone far more intelligent than she had anticipated. She could tell from the way Phillis listened and so quickly picked up words. Phillis was also observed trying to write letters with charcoal outside the house.

In the South, it was against the law to teach a black person to read or write. In the North, it was not against the law, but it was never done. Susannah Wheatley wondered if it might be possible to teach an African to read and write. To learn and understand the Bible. She would try to prove that it was not only white people who could master languages and the arts. Susannah Wheatley was excited by the very notion.

Candle, Quill, and Ink

A candle flickered. Its flame spun a gold cocoon of light in the corner of the room where Phillis sat at a desk, copying Bible passages. Susannah Wheatley was so impressed with Phillis's progress, she had given her books and the tools with which Phillis could study whenever she had spare time—a candle, a quill, and a pot of ink.

Phillis had been in America a mere sixteen months, and within that short time, she had learned not only to speak English but to write it, read the Bible, and understand some of the hardest passages. Many of these she copied down. She was only nine years old and she had already learned more than some white colonial girls and women ever did.

Phillis began with English and then moved on to study Latin and Greek, geography and mathematics. What she enjoyed most, though, was poetry. She liked the clear sharp images, the pictures that poems made in her mind.

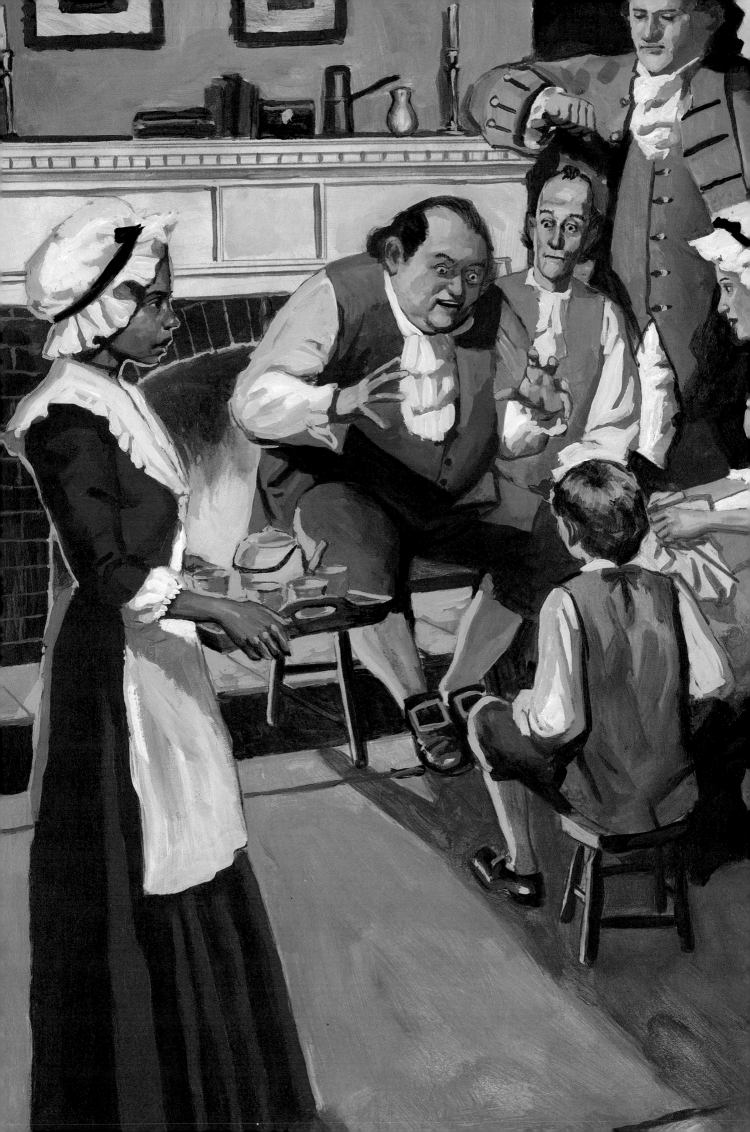

One afternoon in 1765, while serving visitors lunch, Phillis listened to an amazing tale. Mr. Hussey and Mr. Coffin, just arrived from Nantucket, were telling of their terrifying voyage to Boston. Their ship had nearly sunk off Cape Cod in the late winter storm. They described waves as high as mountains, a shrieking wind that tore sails to shreds and that splintered masts. How had the two men survived? Were they scared to death? The images of the two men lashed by the storm began to build in her mind's eye. What a miracle that these same two men now sat safe and warm at the Wheatley table.

Very soon after this, Phillis composed a poem describing Mr. Hussey's and Mr. Coffin's fearful voyage. This poem was published two years later, in 1767, in the newspaper *Newport Mercury*. It is said to be Phillis's very first published poem. Phillis was just fourteen years old.

Susannah Wheatley was stunned. Her little experiment in trying to prove that black people from Africa could read and write had gone beyond her wildest dreams.

She was so excited that she began to take Phillis into the parlors of the finest families in Boston so Phillis could read her poems.

"No, thank you," Phillis would say softly when the mistress of one of these fine houses offered her a place at the tea table. She might then nod toward a smaller table off to the side and offer to sit there. The hostess would usually seem relieved and order her own slaves to set a single place at the side table for the "Negro poet" who had just recited her lovely verses.

One time, however, a hostess and her three daughters, though friendly, became more and more nervous as they realized on which ship this Negro poet had been brought. This was the home of Timothy Fitch. When Phillis herself thought she could not stay another minute and started to leave, Mrs. Fitch fluttered about, insisting that she stay. The daughters sat silently. It was an awful afternoon for everyone.

Phillis was sipping tea in the house of the man who was responsible for her kidnapping. As she watched Mrs. Fitch pour tea from an elegant teapot, maybe she thought of her own mother, pouring water from the calabash in the first light of the morning sun. It was indeed the same sun that shone in both Boston and Africa. And these women were all mothers. Perhaps that was what shocked Phillis most of all. They were all mothers, black or white. But the children of the white ones had not been kidnapped.

With Secret Rage

"Liberty! Property, and no stamps!" The hoarse cries from the mobs in the streets could be heard inside the Wheatley mansion. From their windows, the Wheatley family could see the unruly mob building.

A dozen or more patriots carried a coffin on their shoulders, in which lay an effigy of the newly appointed stamp master of Boston. The people of Boston were seething mad because a new tax by England had been placed upon every newspaper, legal document, letter, announcement—even decks of cards. The mob continued on to the Stamp Building, which they destroyed. Then they rushed to the house of the stamp master and began to smash the windows.

Phillis started to consider the issue of freedom. The colonies in which Phillis lived as a slave were struggling to slip the chains of their own enslavement to England. And from the house on King Street, she was seeing this new struggle erupt.

Phillis began writing about the violence of the streets of Boston and sometimes the violence of being a slave. In her poem "America" she wrote about the Stamp Act that England had placed on her colonies:

"She laid some taxes on her darling son
and would have laid another act there on . . .
Why weeps americus why weeps my child
Thus spake Brittania, thus benign and mild . . ."

The images of America's struggle for freedom and Phillis's kidnapping and enslavement sometimes overlapped within a poem. In one poem, Phillis explains the source of her love of freedom. "I, young in life, was snatch'd from Afric's fancy'd happy seat. . . ." And she still wondered how her parents must have worried: "What sorrows labour in my parents' breast?"

In February of 1770, a mob of angry young patriots surrounded the house of a British informer, who came out with a gun and shot into the crowd. Christopher Snider fell dead, a bullet in his chest. He was eleven years old. The death of a child shocked everyone. Even the British, Phillis thought. And in her poem about the death of Christopher Snider, she wrote about the secret rage in every heart when a child is senselessly murdered. Phillis called Christopher the first martyr of the Revolution.

Two weeks after Christopher Snider's death, there was more violence, more blood, and it all began with a snowball fight right on Phillis's own street, King Street. It was the Boston Massacre. A group of people began throwing snowballs at the British soldiers. One soldier cocked his rifle and shot.

Phillis wrote a poem about the massacre. One of the men who died in the massacre was black, a former slave. His name was Crispus Attucks. He was the first black martyr of the Revolution.

My Phillis

"If he hasn't the impudence to sit upon the same seat with my Phillis!" Susannah Wheatley was fuming as she saw the carriage draw up in front of the house on King Street. Phillis, who suffered from colds and asthma, was sitting on the driver's seat, next to Prince, in the cold weather.

Susannah Wheatley fretted constantly over Phillis's health. Prince was scolded severely for encouraging Phillis to sit beside him, especially in the cold! Phillis felt confused. She sat at side tables, but she was not supposed to sit on the same carriage bench as a Negro. Black on the outside, educated like a white, yet not permitted, except in the Wheatley family, to join whites at the table—was there any place that she really belonged? It seemed to Phillis she was halfway between two worlds. Even in church, which she attended with the Wheatleys, there was a separate place for Negroes to sit.

But still Phillis loved church. She was fascinated by the Reverend George Whitefield, who came from England to preach in America. Mr. Whitefield believed that true Christianity meant love of everyone, "orphans, paupers, Indians, and slaves." The Reverend even went so far as to say that it was sinful for the white man to enslave his black brother. The spiritual world of which George Whitefield spoke—the Christian God that saw no color—was an inspiration for much of Phillis's poetry. Within this spiritual world, Phillis felt free; within her poetry, she felt neither white nor black. When Whitefield died, Phillis was just sixteen. The loss she felt when he died stirred her. Just as the memory of her mother always made her think of the sun, so did that of George Whitefield. He had brought light to the minds of New England people as they worshipped. So, in her mind, Phillis held once again the image of a sun, brilliant and shining. She wrote a poem in honor of George Whitefield.

"Unhappy we thy setting Sun deplore,
Which once was splendid, but it shines no more."

The poem was published as a broadside, or handbill, and read on both sides of the Atlantic—in the colonies and in England. At seventeen Phillis became famous.

The Test

It was a bright spring day in 1772, but inside the courthouse, the air was still cold. Eighteen learned men sat in a semicircle, and Phillis was asked to stand in the middle. The men were well known. They included John Hancock; the governor of the colony, Thomas Hutchinson; the lieutenant governor, Andrew Oliver; a merchant; and a distinguished minister.

Phillis was not greased or naked as she had been when she first arrived in Boston. But, once again, she was to be assessed by white strangers. The men had read the collection of poems Phillis had written, but they did not believe that an African could have written them without help. And yet her mistress—a respectable Christian woman—and her husband said she had. They even wanted the poems published as a book! A book written by a Negro woman! The idea was ridiculous.

Without proof of Phillis's education, the collection of poems could not be published. No one knows what they asked Phillis to do to prove her learning. Perhaps to conjugate Greek verbs, or maybe to recite a poem by the famous English poet John Milton, whom she admired.

But she must have convinced them, for the men wrote that they did indeed believe the poems were written by "Phillis, a young Negro girl, who was but a few years since, brought an uncultivated Barbarian from Africa . . . and now is . . . a slave."

Even with this letter of proof, printers in Boston still refused to publish the work of a Negro. But the Wheatleys would not give up, especially Susannah, who had grown to love Phillis as a daughter. She would fight for her daughter's right to be published—even if it meant sending her to England.

to Meet a King

On May 8, 1773, Phillis Wheatley went to sea for the second time in her life. This was a very different voyage. She was not crouched in the darkness of a stinking cargo hold but enjoyed the privacy of her own cabin. The purpose of her trip was to meet with her publisher and all the English people who had been reading her poems. Many of these people were members of a Christian missionary society and were supporters and close friends of the Reverend George Whitefield. Two of these people, the Countess of Huntington and the Earl of Dartmouth, would use their money and connections to get the book published.

When Phillis Wheatley stepped off the ship in England, it was not onto the auction block of a slave market but into the center of English society. Her patron, the Countess of Huntington, had arranged for Phillis to be received into many fine homes. Everyone wanted to meet the young Negro slave poet from America. Even the king wanted to meet Phillis.

Phillis had been in England a very short time when she received word that Susannah Wheatley was desperately ill. Phillis knew that she must return on the next ship. There was no time to meet the king.

But as short as her trip had been, she knew that something remarkable had occurred. As the sails filled with wind and the English coast faded behind her, she knew that England, the country whose power the colonies resented, had in fact published a slave girl's book—the first book ever written by a black American woman.

Books, Freedom, and Revolution

The colonies themselves were beginning to grow more and more restless in their own enslavement. Four months after Phillis returned to America, one of the men who had doubted her, John Hancock, saw the scheme he himself had masterminded unfold on a chilly night in Boston Harbor. Patriots who were poorly disguised as Native Americans sneaked aboard an English vessel loaded with tea and began dumping the tea into the water.

Phillis could not see the tea party from the house on King Street, but she could hear the whoops and shouts in the room where she tended her ailing mistress. The first copies of Phillis's book were due to arrive any day in the same harbor, now floating with crates of tea.

On January 24, 1774, an advertisement was placed in the *Boston Gazette* announcing the American publication:

This day is published
Adorn'd with an elegant Engraving of the Author
(Price 3s 4d L.M. Bound)
POEMS
On various subjects—Religious and Moral,
By Phillis Wheatley,
a Negro girl
Sold by Mess'rs Cox & Berry
at their store, in King Street, Boston.

The book sold well. Three hundred more copies were ordered, and they arrived on May 6, 1774. Had they arrived three weeks later, they would never have been delivered, for on June 1, by order of the British Parliament, Boston Harbor was blockaded. The Revolution was about to begin. The British sent more troops to Boston. Redcoats were quartered in all the houses, including the Wheatleys'.

The blockade made for shortages. England was trying to starve the colonies into submission. But the fishing port of Marblehead, north of Boston, sent codfish; nearby Charlestown shared its stash of rice; and Baltimore, far to the south, sent bread and whiskey. Patriots as far away as Connecticut walked with a flock of 258 sheep to Boston. Poetry was the last thing on any colonist's mind. But Phillis kept writing.

Susannah Wheatley died that spring, but she had lived long enough to see Phillis succeed. She and Mr. Wheatley had given Phillis her manumission papers, freeing her from slavery within weeks of her return from England. But Phillis had no intention of leaving the household that had nurtured her.

The Poet's Voice

A candle burned as Phillis sat alone in her bedroom. The images began to gather in her head, as once more the light of the rising sun crept over the edge of the land. There was again the figure of her mother carrying the calabash, the plains of Africa reaching endlessly, with their tall grass bending in the wind. The same wind that blew the ships — with their pale white sails like birds of prey — that came to snatch her away.

Phillis let the image of the sun fill her mind. She was trying to write a reply to a poem that an English navy officer had written to her. A new law had forced the people of Boston to give English soldiers lodgings, and two were quartered at the Wheatley house. She was trying to explain to the officer where she had come from. Phillis was trying to recall Africa's beauty, for after all, the same sun shone both there and here, and in England. She must bring the pictures in her mind to these gentlemen who had come on the king's business of bending America to his will. She must, for she was a poet.

EPILOGUE

A year after Phillis Wheatley wrote the poem "Reply" to the English naval officer, she met George Washington, commander of the Continental Army. General Washington was headquartered with his troops in Cambridge, Massachusetts. Phillis had written to him previously, including a poem entitled "To His Excellency General Washington."

In his reply to her of February 28, 1776, he addressed her as "Miss Phillis." It is thought by scholars that this might be the first time in George Washington's life that he addressed a Negro woman as "Miss." In March of that year, the poet and the general met in Cambridge. The poem she had written to him was published the following month in the *Pennsylvania Magazine*, then edited by Thomas Paine.

In 1778 Phillis married John Peters, a struggling black businessman. She bore him three children, all of whom died in infancy. By 1783 the American Revolution had ended, and in 1784 Phillis Wheatley wrote her final poem, "Liberty and Peace," which celebrated the end of the war. Phillis Wheatley died nearly penniless in a boarding house in Boston that same year. She was only thirty-one years old, but she had made an indelible mark on American literature.

AUTHOR'S NOTE

As an author, I was drawn to the story of Phillis Wheatley because I felt it was not simply the story of an illiterate slave girl who became a poet, but rather a story about voice and the relationship between voice, identity, and freedom. What slavery and every other form of oppression have in common is that they impose silence. To be voiceless is to be dehumanized. That was one of the reasons slaves were not permitted to learn how to read and write. We are all diminished as human beings—not simply as a race but as members of a species—when we are silenced. Phillis's first liberation came when she learned to read and write and discovered her own voice as a poet. Her second liberation came when she was handed her manumission papers.

ILLUSTRATOR'S NOTE

I was inspired by the story of Phillis Wheatley because it is an extraordinary tale of America. This young slave woman overcame a traumatic kidnapping, the harsh journey over the Middle Passage to America, and the horror of being sold into slavery. She became a published poet at a time when education for slaves was forbidden. Phillis Wheatley proved to everyone around her that all things are possible if you work for them, and that with freedom, any goal can be accomplished.

A facsimile of the frontispiece to Phillis Wheatley's one published book, *Poems on Various Subjects, Religious and Moral.* This edition held at the Massachusetts Historical Society and reproduced here with permission.

To my family, the Bridwells
P. L.

Page 39: Title page and frontispiece of *Poems on Various Subjects, Religious and Moral* by Phillis Wheatley (London: A. Bell, 1773). Reprinted by permission of the Massachusetts Historical Society.

Endpapers: Letter to Mary Wooster, 15 July 1778 by Phillis Wheatley. Hugh Upham Clark Papers. Reprinted by permission of the Massachusetts Historical Society.

First edition 2003

Library of Congress Cataloging-in-Publication Data

Lasky, Kathryn.
Phillis Wheatley / Kathryn Lasky ; illustrated by Paul Lee.
p.   cm.
Summary: A biography of an African girl brought to New England as a slave in 1761 who became famous on both sides of the Atlantic as the first black woman poet in America.
ISBN 0-7636-0252-3
1. Wheatley, Phillis, 1753–1784—Juvenile literature. 2. Poets, American—18th century—Biography—Juvenile literature. 3. African-American women poets—Biography—Juvenile literature. 4. Slaves—United States—Biography—Juvenile literature. [1. Wheatley, Phillis, 1753–1784. 2. Poets, American. 3. Slaves. 4. African Americans—Biography. 5. Women—Biography.] I. Lee, Paul, ill. II. Title.
PS866.W5 Z65 2003
811'.1—dc21
[B]   2001047139

2 4 6 8 10 9 7 5 3 1

Printed in Italy

This book was typeset in Columbus MT.
The illustrations were done in acrylic on board.

Candlewick Press
2067 Massachusetts Avenue
Cambridge, Massachusetts 02140

visit us at www.candlewick.com